CONTENTS

THE SNOW L[A

By Debi Gliori

CW00956374

ABOUT THE SERIES
INSIDE FRONT COVER

BACKGROUND INFORMATION
3–5

LESSON PLANS
6–22

PHOTOCOPIABLES
23–32

SKILLS GRID
INSIDE BACK COVER

CREDITS

Published by Scholastic Ltd,
Villiers House,
Clarendon Avenue,
Leamington Spa,
Warwickshire CV32 5PR
Text © Anne Washtell
© 1997 Scholastic Ltd
1 2 3 4 5 6 7 8 9 0   7 8 9 0 1 2 3 4 5 6

Author Anne Washtell
Series Consultant Fiona Collins
Editor Clare Gallaher
Assistant Editor Lesley Sudlow
Series designer Lynne Joesbury
Designer Claire Belcher
Illustrations Kim Woolley and Debi Gliori
Cover illustration Debi Gliori

Designed using Adobe Pagemaker

British Library Cataloguing-in-Publication Data
A catalogue record for this book is available from the British Library.

ISBN 0-590-54708-9

ACKNOWLEDGEMENTS

Debi Gliori for five new illustrations (pages 24, 25, 29, 31) based on *The Snow Lambs* by Debi Gliori. Text © 1995, Debi Gliori. Additional illustrations © 1998, Debi Gliori.
A & C Black Ltd for the use of a text extract from 'Snow is Falling' by Franklyn M Branley from *First Sight Series* © Franklyn M Branley, A & C Black.
Marian Reiner (Literary Agent), New York for the author for the use of 'Wind Song' by Lilian Moore from *I Feel The Same Way* by Lilian Moore © 1967, renewed 1995, Lilian Moore.
Every effort has been made to trace copyright holders and the publishers apologize for any inadvertent omissions.

BACKGROUND INFORMATION

GENRE

The Snow Lambs, written and illustrated by Debi Gliori, is a beautiful, multi-layered picture book in which text and illustrations work together to tell a realistic, emotionally rewarding tale about the relationship between a boy and his dog. Although most children will find the lifestyle of Sam and his family a sharp contrast to their own, they will relate to his fears and will be able to share his anxieties about his lost dog. They will also begin to appreciate how weather can so strongly affect people's lives. The illustrations carry much of the underlying meaning of the story and depict the rural and domestic settings in contrasting detail. Because they are such an important feature of the book, they are well worth careful study in their own right.

PLOT SUMMARY

The Snow Lambs, set in a remote, hill farm location, is all about the courage of a faithful sheepdog called Bess who rescues a stray ewe and bravely leads it back to the safety of the farmhouse. In the course of their adventures, Bess and the ewe have to endure the most severe wintry weather conditions. They also have to overcome their fear at the height of the storm, when the electricity power lines are brought down by an old elm tree as it crashes to the ground. However, the story ends happily, with the ewe giving birth to twin lambs and Bess being joyfully reunited with the farmer's son, Sam.

Crucial to the plot is that the story of *The Snow Lambs* is much more than this brief outline; it is in fact two parallel stories cleverly woven into one. Through the skilful use of the text but especially through the power of her illustrations, Debi Gliori also tells the story of Sam, the farmer's son who is Bess's loving and loyal friend. Sam's anxieties and fears for Bess's safety are conveyed within the setting of the warmth, security, light and comfort of the farmhouse. The contrast between the setting of Sam's story and the harsh, dark, cold and frightening world that Bess is inhabiting outside could not be more marked.

As the story reaches its climax, both their worlds become merged by the terrifying ferocity of the storm. This proves to be the turning point in the story, and all turns out well in the final pages, with the safe return of Bess and the ewe, and the birth of the 'snow lambs'.

ABOUT THE AUTHOR/ILLUSTRATOR

Debi Gliori is half Italian and half Scottish. When she left school, Debi planned to become an astrophysicist, but after giving birth to her eldest child she decided to go to art college instead and learn how to become an illustrator. Since 1984, she has been a full-time illustrator and writer, and lives in the countryside near Edinburgh with her two sons and daughter. She has written several other books, including *Lion at Bedtime* which, like *The Snow Lambs*, has a strong appeal for younger readers.

SPECIFIC TEACHING OPPORTUNITIES

TEXT LEVEL

The Snow Lambs offers a wealth of opportunities for working at text level, with the illustrations also clearly contributing much in terms of additional layers of meaning to the written text. The structure of the story can be explored and sequenced in the way the parallel stories of Sam and Bess are told in words and pictures. The juxtaposition of the bitter cold outdoor story of Bess and the warm, cosy inside story of Sam enables comparisons to be made between the settings, and can lead to discussions on key themes within the book, for example the relationship between people and their animals, the influence of weather on our lives, and what causes us to be anxious and fearful. This can lead to a more detailed examination of the plot and the characters, with opportunities given for retelling the story in both oral and written form, and through role-play.

SENTENCE LEVEL

Many of the lesson plans and photocopiable sheets require work to be undertaken at sentence level, both in reading and writing. For example, lesson plans involving role-play help them to distinguish between spoken and written language and to look at how punctuation can be used to create particular effects. Children are given the opportunity to increase their awareness of how sentences appear to the reader, for example by looking at devices such as the capitalization of complete words in sentences to provide emphasis. At a deeper level, they are encouraged to see how authors indicate the difference between words that are spoken aloud and words that are thought, which also increases their understanding of the story as a whole.

WORD LEVEL

One of the strengths of *The Snow Lambs* is Debi Gliori's choice of vocabulary. The text provides a rich resource for a wide range of word-level work, including examining the structure and patterning of words, studying differences in their spelling, analysing and explaining variations in the sound and spelling of rhyming words, searching for descriptive language and interpreting metaphors. Discussion of the role of the illustrations in structuring the parallel stories leads into work on contrasts and antonyms. The book allows for many opportunities for the children to search for specific words and phrases within the text and then discuss similarities and differences in their meaning.

READING THE TEXT

The pages of *The Snow Lambs* are not numbered. However, in order to link specific lesson plans to particular pages in the story, a straightforward numbering system has been used in this book, starting with the title page as page 1, the dedication page as page 2 and so on. The final page of the story text is page 32.
Note: It is suggested for ease of reference that you use small, numbered Post-it notes to mark the pages before using the lesson plans.

The Snow Lambs can be divided into three clear sections: pages 3–9, pages 10–20 and pages 21–32. The majority of the lesson plans fall within one or more of these sections, so it may be helpful if you have indicated the sections prior to using the book. In order to achieve specific objectives within the Literacy Hour, it has been necessary to take chunks of the book as a focus for the lesson plans. However, it is important to avoid the children's experience of *The Snow Lambs* becoming fragmented, and for this reason the children should also hear complete readings of the book to maintain the full message of the story.

BIG BOOK

A Big Book version of *The Snow Lambs* is available from Scholastic Ltd. This is an ideal resource for use in the whole-class sessions, as the teacher-led elements of the lesson plans which focus on the specifics of text and/or illustrations are made much easier to undertake through its use. Not only does the Big Book ensure that all children can see *The Snow Lambs* properly but it enables the teacher to promote active participation and interaction with the text by the children. Most importantly, the teacher can use the Big Book for demonstration purposes. It also allows the teacher to draw attention to crucial details in the illustrations which the children might miss in their independent work.

ABOUT THE POSTER

SIDE I
This side of the poster links to the cold weather theme of the book and provides extracts from three different genres: fiction (a quote from *The Snow Lambs*), non-fiction (a passage about snow) and poetry ('Wind Song' by Lilian Moore). It should be used to enable children to compare and contrast the different types of text (see 'Different kinds of text' on page 10) and to help to clarify important details in the book concerning problems encountered when the effects of winter weather are felt by people and animals (see 'Role-play: understanding an incident' on page 13).

SIDE 2
This supports the sheep-farming setting of the story and is intended to give children the opportunity to be introduced to specific vocabulary to do with sheep (see 'Lambs and lambing' on page 20). It also includes a well-known saying, linking shepherds with weather, and a traditional sheep-counting rhyme.

LINKED RESOURCES

OTHER BOOKS BY DEBI GLIORI
The Snowchild (Frances Lincoln)
Little Bear and the Wish Fish (Frances Lincoln)
Mr Bear Babysits (Orchard Books)
Mr Bear to the Rescue (Walker Books)
Lion at Bedtime (Picture Hippo)

OTHER BOOKS WITH A SIMILAR THEME
The Sheep-Pig by Dick King-Smith (Puffin)
Animal Ark: Sheepdog in the Snow by Lucy Daniels (Hodder Children's Books)
Jess the Border-collie titles including *The Arrival, The Challenge* and *The Runaway* by Lucy Daniels (Hodder Children's Books)
The stories about *Floss and the Shepherd Boy* by Kim Lewis (Walker Books)
Farm, from the Eyewitness Guide series (Dorling Kindersley)
Weather by Brian Cosgrove, from the Eyewitness Guide series (Dorling Kindersley)
Weather, from the Eyewitness Explorers series (Dorling Kindersley)
Nursery rhymes featuring sheep/lambs: *The Puffin Book of Nursery Rhymes* edited by Iona and Peter Opie (Puffin)
Poems on winter: *A Very First Poetry Book* and *A First Poetry Book* (OUP)

OTHER RESOURCES
Shared Reading, Shared Writing (Centre for Language in Primary Education)
The Lake District: Life and Traditions by William Rollinson (Weidenfeld & Nicholson)
The Good Guide to the Lakes by Hunter Davies (Forster Davies)

LESSON PLANS

FIRST IMPRESSIONS

RESOURCES NEEDED

Other picture books by Debi Gliori (for display purposes), photocopiable pages 23 and 24, dictionaries, photocopies of the front cover (one per pair), flip chart or whiteboard, writing and drawing materials.

WHOLE-CLASS WORK

In this lesson plan the children will learn that the front cover firmly establishes the two main characters in the story and the warmth of their special relationship. It also gives strong visual indications about the setting and plot of the story (the adverse weather conditions). The title itself provides additional information as to what the story is all about, and in so doing entices the reader to open the book in order to find out more.

Show the children *The Snow Lambs*, ensuring that they can all see the front cover, and ask them questions which will elicit their first impressions of what the book might be about. Draw attention to the main characters by asking the children who they can see in the illustration. Who do they think the dog might belong to and why does the boy seems to be hugging him so tightly? Ask the children to comment on the boy's clothes, and link his appearance and the snow on the front cover to the severity of the weather conditions.

Encourage the children to talk about their own experiences of being outside in snowy weather. Did they enjoy it and what clothes did they wear in order to keep warm? Extend their contributions by encouraging them to think of words or phrases that could be used to describe the cold, snowy weather (such as *snowflakes, snowstorm*) and how they might be feeling physically (such as *shivering, cold*). Return to the illustration on the front cover, asking them to speculate on why the boy and the dog are out in the snow, and list their ideas on the flip chart.

Next, focus on the print by discussing the title of the book and introducing the author. Have the children heard of Debi Gliori before or any other books written by her? Provide some background information on the author and draw attention to the classroom display of books by Debi Gliori. Discuss with the children why they think the author decided to call her book *The Snow Lambs*. What do they think the 'snow lambs' might be and, more importantly, what connection could the 'snow lambs' have with the boy and his dog?

GROUP WORK

In mixed ability groups, ask the children to predict from the title what they think the story is going to be about. Give each child a copy of photocopiable page 23, *The Snow Lambs* (1)', and distribute copies of the cover. Before the children start working on the photocopiable sheet, read the title of the book aloud as a reminder. Explain that they can carry out an initial brainstorm of ideas in their groups before filling in the sheet individually. Once the sheet has been completed, the children can compare their predictions in their groups, which will help them with the reporting-back stage in the plenary session.

EXTENSION

Ask the children to move on to photocopiable page 24, *The Snow Lambs* (2)', which focuses on extending vocabulary in relation to the title. (Where appropriate, they should be encouraged to use dictionaries to extend their word list.)

PLENARY

Ask the groups to report back in turn to discuss their predictions. To maximize efficient use of time, ask them to indicate only those ideas that were similar to other people's. List the key points on the flip chart, if possible categorizing the responses or tallying similar predictions. Having heard the other groups' predictions, summarize the 'evidence' so far for the children. Which prediction do they as a whole class feel is most likely to be an accurate description of what happens in the story? Finally, make a list of their alternative titles for the book.

WHAT'S THIS STORY ALL ABOUT?

RESOURCES NEEDED

Big Book version of *The Snow Lambs* (or enlarged copies of pages 3–6), photocopiable page 25, flip chart or whiteboard, writing materials.

WHOLE-CLASS WORK

This lesson plan enables children to take a look at the plot of *The Snow Lambs* for the first time. Pages 3–6 provide an excellent opportunity to demonstrate how the illustrations and text work together to convey the deeper meaning of the story. During their earliest encounters with the book, it is important that the children are encouraged to see the value of looking for additional information about the story through the illustrations. Not only do the illustrations confirm the meaning of the story, they also frequently add further layers of detail and sometimes carry a different message from the text. Some pages of *The Snow Lambs* contain no text at all. The message of the story is borne solely by the illustrations.

Write the heading 'What's this story all about?' on the flip chart. Working first at text level, show the class *The Snow Lambs* and explain that they will be looking at the first few pages of the story in order to find out more about the book. Then, through shared reading, read aloud pages 3 and 4, stopping at 'I wonder where Bess is, he thought'. Turn back to page 3 and show the children how each sentence can be matched to an element of the illustration.

Then use questions to help the children examine the illustrations further, to provide more evidence about what Sam and his father are doing and the reasons for their actions. Ask why they are counting the sheep. Have all the sheep stayed together? What is Bess (the sheepdog) doing? Monitor the children's responses and write those points that add information beyond what is given in the text onto the flip chart.

Re-read the responses collated on the flip chart, drawing attention to the fact that one sheep appears to have strayed (page 5) and that the weather conditions are very bad. Use some of the children's responses to model, through shared writing, how their answers to the questions can be recorded in full sentences. A sample sentence might read 'I think *The Snow Lambs* is about a sheep who got lost'. (This will provide a rehearsal for one of the activities in the group work.)

To conclude this part of the lesson plan, tell the children that they will now be looking at page 4 and the next two pages of the book themselves to find out more about the story.

LESSON PLANS

GROUP WORK

Place the children into differentiated groups, organized in pairs. Ask them to look at the double-page spread on pages 4 and 5. Tell the children to first read through the text together and match the text on page 4 to the pictures. Then they should read the text on page 6, look carefully again at the illustrations on all three pages, and focus on the following key questions:

* Why is Sam's dad looking so worried?
* What do you think Bess, the sheepdog, is doing?

Depending on the independence of the groups, it may help to give the children the questions one at a time.

Encourage the children, working in their pairs, to find as many possible answers to the questions as they can. Explain that they should agree on the wording of their best answers before writing them down on a copy of photocopiable page 25, 'What's this story all about?' They should aim to write their answers in full sentences. A lead-in phrase, such as 'I think Sam's dad is worried because...' could be written onto the sheet to provide support for children who need it.

When the children have answered the first two questions, ask them to look at the illustration on page 5 and try to answer the third question on the sheet:

* Why do you think they would be in trouble if the tree blew down across the power lines?

As the pairs complete the task, they should compare their findings with the other pairs in their group and agree on all the different answers that they can offer in the report back in the plenary session.

PLENARY

Ask each group to report back on their agreed answers to the three questions that they wrote down on the photocopiable sheet in the group activity. For the first two questions, monitor in their responses their use of detail from the illustrations. For example, in response to question 1, do they refer to the weather (the snow and the wind), the tree that looks as though it is about to fall onto the power lines, and the branches in the river? In response to question 2, do they notice that Bess is watching the sheep who has crossed to the other side of the river? Clarify points as necessary (it is quite possible that the children may not pick up on the significance of the 'power lines'; the specific vocabulary may also be unfamiliar to them). Draw out key points in relation to the development of the plot. In their answers to question 3, do they know that the tree blowing down across the power lines would cut off the electricity and plunge the characters at home into darkness?

Finally, discuss their answers briefly and link them back to the original question 'What's this story all about?'

THE WEATHER'S MOODS

RESOURCES NEEDED

Flip chart or whiteboard, photocopiable page 26, dictionaries, writing materials, illustrated weather word bank (optional).

WHOLE-CLASS WORK

This lesson plan aims to draw the children's attention to the key role of the weather in the setting of *The Snow Lambs*. At text level, the children will identify the different elements of the weather and will be listening to and looking out for weather words and phrases. They will also use information from the illustrations to expand their vocabulary further. At word level, the focus will be on how nouns and adjectives work together when a section of the text is explored for the identification of weather words and phrases. This will lead into the children generating some more 'weather phrases' for themselves.

Start by asking the children to think about what sort of weather is described in *The Snow Lambs*. Hold up the front cover of the book, and read out the title. Ask the children which word in the title provides information about the weather. Briefly establish their first impressions concerning the weather in the book and note these on the flip chart.

Now ask the class to listen out for and look for clues about the weather as the first section of book is read (pages 3–9). On completing the reading, ask the children to think of individual words that they have just heard or seen that tell them about the weather. Ask them in pairs to quickly share their ideas and then to report back their list of weather words. List the words on the flip chart but sort them into categories (words that describe clouds, words that describe the wind, words that describe snow and words that describe the cold).

To move into word-level work, take one of the categories, for example the clouds, and read back through the text (pages 3–9), asking the children to stop you when they hear or read any words to do with clouds. This should happen on page 4. Draw attention to the phrase 'storm clouds'. Point to it in the book and look for it on the flip chart list. Explain that the word 'storm' has been used to tell the reader more about the 'clouds'. Hold the book up so that the children can see the illustrations on pages 4 and 5. Ask them to look at the picture of the clouds. Demonstrate how the illustrations can suggest other descriptive words to us, such as 'grey clouds', 'dark clouds' or 'heavy clouds'. Then repeat the procedure using the word 'snow', but this time ask the children to offer some describing words. It may be necessary to prompt them with questions such as, 'What colour is the snow?' or 'Is the snow falling lightly or heavily?'

GROUP WORK

For this activity, which is well suited to ability grouping, give each child a copy of photocopiable page 26, 'Weather words', and explain that, after re-reading the opening section (pages 3–9) of the book to themselves, their task is to find words and phrases that can fit into the four categories given on the photocopiable sheet and write them down. Then they should use the illustrations in the first section of the book to think of more descriptive words and phrases and add them to the sheet, being careful to choose the correct category each time. Encourage the children to use dictionaries to find more descriptive words. Provide those who find the task challenging with a previously prepared, illustrated weather word bank to help them.

The organization of this group work can be flexible. For example, each group could work with a different type of weather (one group working on windy words, one on snowy words and so on) or, within a group, pairs or individuals could work on different elements and then pool their findings on an enlarged copy of the photocopiable sheet.

The final part of the photocopiable sheet asks the children how they would feel if they were Sam out in such cold weather. Again, the book will provide them with clues both in the text and in the pictures.

LESSON PLANS

When the children are finding weather words to complete the photocopiable sheet, suggest that they extend their noun phrases with more adjectives, for example *blinding, heavy, white snow.*

PLENARY

Ask children who have created additional descriptive words and phrases successfully to explain how they achieved this. Take one element of the weather and show the children again how we can take a word such as *wind* and use other words to describe it, for example *fierce wind, cold wind* and *strong wind.* Explain that we call the words that describe the wind 'adjectives'. To conclude, explore with the children how Debi Gliori's use of descriptive language and illustrations about the weather affects us as readers. Ask the children how they would feel if they were Sam.

DIFFERENT KINDS OF TEXT

RESOURCES NEEDED

The poster (Cold, windy weather), flip chart (with page ruled with three vertical columns), photocopiable page 27, writing materials.

WHOLE-CLASS WORK

This lesson plan intends to draw attention to some of the key linguistic features of three different types of text and to show how different texts perform different functions. The unifying theme of cold, windy weather is used as a context, and the language of *The Snow Lambs* is set against that of a poem and an extract from an information book.

As an introduction to the lesson plan, re-read the opening pages of *The Snow Lambs* up to the end of page 6. Then show the 'Cold, windy weather' side of the poster to the children, explaining that it has three pieces of text that all deal with the same subject – cold and windy weather – but that they are written in different ways.

FICTION

Read aloud the sentence under the fiction heading (this is taken from page 6 of the book): 'The wind felt full of sharp little teeth, nibbling at Sam's nose and biting his ears.' Ask the children how they would feel if they were Sam. Can they find the key words and phrases that tell us how cold it is? Can they identify how Debi Gliori has cleverly made the wind behave in a special way (that it has been personified)?

POETRY

Show the children the poem 'Wind Song' by Lilian Moore. Can they identify, just by looking at the layout, what kind of writing it is? If they identify the layout as that of a poem, ask how they know this. (Discuss some features of the layout such as line length and then find some of the rhyming words.)

Before reading the poem through together, ask the children to think about the poem's message while they read. On completing the first read, ask them about the strength of the wind. Can they identify key words and phrases that describe its strength? Then ask them if they can recognize any words and phrases that are the same as or similar to ones they have heard in *The Snow Lambs*. (The children may pick up on words such as *whisper, sky, creak, blows* and *wires on poles*.) List the words that they identify, writing them in the middle column of the prepared sheet on the flip chart.

Turn to page 4 of the story and re-read it to the class so that they can hear these similar words and phrases in a different context. List the similar words in the first column on the chart. Then compare similarities between the windswept trees, in the illustration near to the poem on the poster, and the old elm on page 5 of the book.

NON-FICTION

Let the children look at the short information extract on the poster entitled *Snow is Falling*. What is this piece of writing about? Do they know what kind of book it is from? Compare this extract with the poem and then the sentence from *The Snow Lambs*. The children should be able to identify the common theme but notice that the third text is telling us facts. What does this extract teach us? Finally, summarize for the children that the three text types are: story, poem and non-fiction (information) text.

GROUP WORK

With children working in their differentiated groups, choose the most appropriate task for each group from the following activities:

✳ Give the children copies of photocopiable page 27, 'Snow facts', and ask them to read through the information extract. Explain that they should then read page 4 of *The Snow Lambs* and compare the two extracts, underlining words and phrases in the information text that are similar to words in *The Snow Lambs*. They can also look elsewhere in the book to search for other similar words and list them on a separate sheet of paper.

✳ Ask the children to read aloud the poem 'Wind Song' from the poster and then find all the pairs of rhymes, writing them down in a list. The poem has an unusual rhyme scheme, and they should identify those that have the same spelling pattern and those that do not.

✳ Tell the children to imagine how the wind in *The Snow Lambs* looked as it nibbled and bit Sam. Ask them to make a neat copy of the sentence from the fiction section of the poster and then illustrate it to show how the wind would look.

PLENARY

Ask the information-text group to report back first. Which words in their text did they also find in *The Snow Lambs*? As they supply the words, scribe them onto the third column on the flip chart. Point out to the children that the three pieces of text had many words in common and yet they were written in very different ways. Can the information-text group suggest some of the differences? Why do we use information books?

Next, using the poster, ask the poetry group to report back on their findings about the rhyme scheme of the poem. Ask them to identify the words that were exact rhymes and then focus on those that were 'near miss' rhymes. Take one of the 'near miss' pairs such as *sigh* and *sky* in order to discuss briefly other words that follow these two spelling patterns (such as *high* and *my*).

Finally, give a short summary of the similarities between the three texts and some of the significant differences.

LESSON PLANS

EXPLORING FEELINGS THROUGH TEXT AND PICTURES

RESOURCES NEEDED

Flip chart (with the first sentence of page 13, 'Mum wrapped Sam up...' and then the question 'How is Sam feeling?' written on the first page; the remainder of the text on page 13 and then the question 'How is Sam feeling now?' written on the next page), photocopiable page 28, writing materials, an enlarged colour picture of a cocoon (optional).

WHOLE-CLASS WORK

The aim of this lesson plan is to explore feelings, both physical and emotional, that can be portrayed through text and pictures, with the focus on Sam and his feelings about Bess.

Read the first two sections of *The Snow Lambs* (up to page 20). During the reading, ask the children to think carefully about how Sam is feeling, especially about Bess. After completing the reading, go back to page 13 and tell the children that you are going to re-read the first sentence on the page. Using the illustrations, ask the children what Debi Gliori means by 'Mum wrapped Sam up in the cocoon of a warm towel, then dried his hair'. Have they ever felt snug and warm when they have been wrapped up in a towel? What does the author mean by the word *cocoon*? Have they heard it before? What clues can they find in the pictures and the other words in the sentence? (Use the enlarged picture of a cocoon, as necessary.)

So how is Sam feeling? List the children's words and phrases on the flip chart, for example 'Sam is feeling warm', 'Sam is feeling cosy', 'Sam is feeling...' Draw attention to the cat and ask how it is feeling. Comment on the comfortable, warm cushion that it is relaxing on. Now move on to the remaining text on the page and focus on Sam's question and his mother's answer:

'That's quite a storm brewing out there,' said Mum.
'Will Bess be blown away?' asked Sam.
'Don't worry, Sam. Bess can look after herself,' replied Mum. (page 13)

Incorporating earlier points listed on the flip chart, explain to the children that although Sam is feeling warm and snug on the outside, he might not be feeling the same on the inside. Using the phrase 'Sam is feeling...' as a starter, list down the children's responses on the flip chart. Use questions to extend their ideas. For example, if they say 'Sam is feeling worried', ask 'Why?' Discuss the illustration on page 12 to help extend their responses.

Next, briefly draw the children's attention to the two lists about Sam's feelings which have been compiled on the flip chart and help them to compare and summarize the contradictory feelings that he is experiencing.

Look at page 13 with the children to show them the words on the page that indicate that someone is speaking, such as 'said Mum', 'asked Sam' and 'replied Mum'. Explain that these kinds of words can also tell us when someone is thinking. Turn to page 15 and read out the sentence 'I hope Bess doesn't have to dig her way home, thought Sam, digging out his pyjamas'. Explain that the word 'thought' tells us that these private words are in Sam's mind or inside his head and are not spoken aloud.

Through shared writing, compose two sentences that demonstrate the difference between saying words and thinking them.

LESSON PLANS

GROUP WORK

Place the children into differentiated groups and ask them to read through pages 15–19 to themselves. These pages take Sam's growing anxiety for Bess, and explore it further, telling the reader his hopes and his fears. Each page of text contains Sam's thoughts, signalled by the phrase: 'I hope...' Ask the children to look for three sentences which start with the words 'I hope...' and then to write the sentences down on a copy of photocopiable page 28, 'I hope...'.

More able children can re-read the three sentences and decide which two sentences are Sam's thoughts and which sentence is actually spoken by him. They should fill in the answer on the photocopiable sheet.

Finally, explain that all the children should look back through the story and write down some of their own personal hopes for Bess. These can be written in the thought bubbles on the sheet.

EXTENSION

Tell the children to look again at the complete text on page 13 and find all the proper nouns. They should list the names down and check that each one starts with a capital letter.

PLENARY

Ask the children to recall the three 'I hope...' sentences that they identified in the group activity. Then ask those who pinpointed which sentence was spoken out loud to explain how they worked it out. Pick up on the word *thought* and the word *whispered* and discuss how thoughts remain silent inside our heads, but whispers are spoken words. Talk about why Sam can only whisper his third hope for Bess. Finally, ask the children to share some of their own personal hopes for Bess.

ROLE-PLAY: UNDERSTANDING AN INCIDENT

RESOURCES NEEDED

Big Book version of *The Snow Lambs* (or enlarged copies of page 6), photocopiable page 29, sets of decorated paper plates on thin sticks (to represent Bess, the ewe, Mum, Dad and Sam), flip chart or whiteboard, writing materials.

WHOLE-CLASS WORK

The Snow Lambs reaches its climax on pages 22–23. The storm has reached its peak (on the following page the reader learns that the elm tree has fallen down onto the power lines, cutting off the electricity) and the story of Bess and the ewe and the parallel story of Sam and his family come closer together, the storm affecting all the characters in an intense way. The flash of electrical power splits the illustration down the middle, and shows the characters on each side frozen in their fear. The flash is not referred to in the text, and it is therefore important that the children understand the significance of it in order to fully comprehend the story. By looking at the incident through role-play in this lesson plan, the children will explore the intensity of the feelings experienced by the characters and put these feelings into speech.

To provide a lead-in to the impact of the double-page spread on pages 22–23, re-read *The Snow Lambs* from page 11. At the end of page 21, stop and ask the children to predict what will happen on the next few pages. List their predictions on the flip chart.

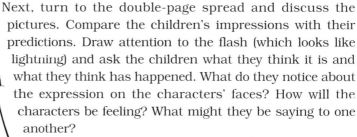

Next, turn to the double-page spread and discuss the pictures. Compare the children's impressions with their predictions. Draw attention to the flash (which looks like lightning) and ask the children what they think it is and what they think has happened. What do they notice about the expression on the characters' faces? How will the characters be feeling? What might they be saying to one another?

Ask five children to stand at the front of the classroom and make a freeze-frame of this point in the story when the flash is seen as the elm tree brings down the power lines. Explain that they should 'freeze' as the characters in the pictures. Briefly, use the role-play to elicit examples of what each character might be saying. Taking the ewe and Bess first, give the children an example, such as 'Help, help!' or 'I'm frightened!' (Develop this as necessary.) Then through shared writing, scribe some examples on the flip chart, writing the spoken text in speech bubbles.

Next, focus on Sam and his parents. What might they be saying to each other? Again, give an example (such as 'Mum, I'm SCARED!' and 'So am I!') but this time demonstrate on the flip chart how we can capitalize words to create emphasis. Discuss the use of exclamation marks and speech marks.

Speech marks: It is important for the children to understand that speech marks are used to help us to identify (or mark) spoken language within continuous written text. Turn to page 6 in the Big Book and point out how speech marks are 'opened' as a character starts to talk and 'closed' when he or she has finished speaking. Draw their attention to the phrases 'said Dad' and 'said Sam', explaining that they signify who has finished speaking. Read some other passages from the Big Book, and ask the children to tell you when someone starts speaking. How do they know? Repeat the procedure, this time asking them to tell you when someone has finished speaking. For more able children, point out the placing of punctuation at the end of a stretch of speech and the conventions used for the layout of spoken text.

Exclamation marks: Ask the children to re-read page 6 with you and to tell you when they find an exclamation mark. What do they notice about the way the text 'BESS! BESS, COME HERE!' has been written? Explain that the exclamation mark is used in addition to the capital letters to show that the words are being spoken loudly.

GROUP WORK

Place the children into differentiated groups and choose the most appropriate task from the following activities:

✳ Organize groups of children into pairs (ewe and Bess) and threes (Sam and his parents). Tell them to practise a freeze-frame and short dialogue to perform in the plenary. Explain that they should focus on the key event of the book that has been the focus of the whole-class session.

✳ Distribute sets of cut-out characters (made from decorated paper plates and sticks) and ask the children to role-play what their characters might be saying.

Encourage the children to make their characters respond to one another's words. These children should perform a short re-enactment in the plenary session.

❋ Ask more able groups to complete copies of photocopiable page 29, 'What did they say?', writing the characters' words in the speech bubbles. They shouldthen practise reading the spoken text with expression and fluency before incorporating the text from one of the speech bubbles into a sentence using speech marks.

EXTENSION

Allow the children to read on independently in the book and hunt for other sentences which use the exclamation mark. Can they compose a complete text for pages 22 and 23, writing it as a conversation and including exclamation marks and speech marks?

PLENARY

Start with the children who have undertaken the role-play and comment on those who sustain conversation, use expression and respond interactively in their dialogue. Take one short example, and demonstrate on the flip chart how it can be turned into written language.

Invite children who have completed the speech bubbles on the photocopiable sheet to read out their examples. Ask those who have tried writing sentences, using speech marks, capitalization for emphasis and exclamation marks, to talk about their work.

Finally, ask one or two children to read out sentences that they have found in the book which use exclamation marks.

THE PARALLEL STORIES

RESOURCES NEEDED

A set of cards labelled 'inside' and 'outside' (laminated, if possible), flip chart (with a horizontal line dividing the page across the middle and the heading 'Sam's Story' written at the top of the page, and 'Bess's Story' written underneath the line), Blu-Tack, small pieces of card to make a set of 'antonym' cards (see 'Group work'), dictionaries/wordbooks, A4 paper, writing materials.

WHOLE-CLASS WORK

The Snow Lambs charts the parallel stories of Bess and Sam through the interplay of text and illustrations. This lesson plan explores Debi Gliori's skilful use of the juxtaposition of 'warm' and 'cold' frames within the book. These frames alter in size as the story progresses, and the children will discover that these changes reflect the shifting emphasis and eventual convergence of the parallel stories of Bess and Sam. The intention in this lesson plan is to track a part of the parallel stories through a closer look at the illustrations, considering:
❋ the use of frames in the illustrations (why they grow and diminish in size)
❋ the symbolism behind the contrasting colours of the illustrations
❋ the contrasts in the parallel stories of Bess and Sam.

Through charting the subtleties of the illustrations, the children will automatically be involved at word level in the identification of and collection of antonyms (opposites).

Re-read the story up to the end of page 7. Ask the children to look carefully at the illustrations on pages 6 and 7 (where the split from the main story begins). Establish whether the children think there is one illustration or two and draw attention to the white frame. Why is it there? Who is inside it? Who is outside it?

Move on to pages 8–11, looking at each double-page spread and asking the children if they can find the white frames. What or who can they see inside the frames? (Provide direct guidance here if necessary.) As you look through the frames together, draw attention (if the children do not) to the fact that the frames seem to be growing across the page. Follow the patterning of the frames for the children and discuss why this is happening, establishing that the size of the frame is larger if it illustrates the text that is written on the page.

Now record on the flip chart the parallel stories and contrasting experiences of Bess and Sam. Using the set of 'inside' and 'outside' cards, tell the children that you are going to look at the frames again to see what the pictures are telling us about the story. Point out that they may have already noticed that some of the illustrations seem to be inside the house in the warm, while others are outside in the cold.

Starting at pages 6 and 7, go back through the frames, asking the children to decide whether the illustrations are 'inside' or 'outside'. Invite them to fix the appropriate cards onto the frames with Blu-Tack, thus revealing the patterning of the story. Ask the children who is inside the house (Sam and his family) and who is outside (Bess and the ewe). Write the word 'inside' on Sam's side of the line on the flip chart and 'outside' on Bess's side. Use these words to initiate a discussion on antonyms, which should be suggested and listed as appropriate on either side of the line.

Using 'inside' and 'outside' as a focus, discuss contrasts in colour, temperature and feelings between the indoor and outdoor frames. Those to do with feelings may need mediation, such as *safe*, *unsafe*, *secure* and *insecure*. Record the information on the flip chart. Stop at pages 14 and 15 and review the children's findings. Use the evidence on the flip chart to draw out the comparisons and contrasts between Sam's story above the line and Bess's story below the line.

GROUP WORK

With children working in their differentiated groups, choose the most appropriate task for each group from the following activities:

✳ Give the children a set of 'inside'/'outside' and 'warm'/'cold' cards to use with their copies of *The Snow Lambs*. Tell them to turn to page 16, picking up the story at that point, and then choose the appropriate card to fix onto each page, using Blu-Tack, continuing until they reach the end of the book. They should then compare the two sets of cards.

✳ After placing a set of 'warm'/'cold' cards as in the activity above, ask the children to look at the contrasting illustrations in the book that have been labelled with the cards and note down which colours are used for the 'cold' pictures and which colours are used for the 'warm' pictures. They should discuss why this is so and identify connections between them.

✳ Make a set of antonym cards by preparing a set of pairs of opposite words, writing each word on a small piece of card (for example, one pair of cards could have *boy* on one card and *girl* on the other). Take the antonym cards and ask the children to play a game called 'Antonym pairs'. Shuffle the complete set and then place them face down on the table. The first player turns over one card and reads it, then turns over another card. If the words are opposites, the player can retain them as an antonym pair. If the words are not opposites, the cards are returned face down to their original position, and the next child has a turn. When all the cards have been picked up, the player who has the most antonym pairs wins.

✳ Children who have played the 'Antonym pairs' game above can then go on to make an additional list of antonyms, using dictionaries or wordbooks and working in pairs. Start off the list for them using a pair of words that has not been used in the game. Who can make the longest list?

LESSON PLANS

PLENARY

Ask the group who has been working with the 'warm' and 'cold' and 'inside' and 'outside' cards to compare a few pages of the parallel text. Did they follow the same patterning with their cards? Why?

Ask the children who looked at the different colours used in the illustrations to make a statement about the colour choices made by Debi Gliori. They might say, for example: 'The warm pictures used lots of orange, red and yellow...'

Invite the children who played the 'Antonym pairs' game and completed a list of antonyms to share their list of words. Can the class add some more antonyms arising from their work with *The Snow Lambs* or by remembering other antonyms that they know?

Finally, review the evidence gathered from the illustrations about the stories of Bess and Sam.

THE STORY OF BESS AND THE EWE

RESOURCES NEEDED

Big Book version of *The Snow Lambs* (or flip chart with pages showing quick sketches of the opening 'cold' frames of the story), photocopiable page 30, Blu-Tack, scissors, glue sticks, blank booklets for stories or sheets of A4 paper, dictionaries, writing materials.

WHOLE-CLASS WORK

In this lesson plan, the children work with illustrations of Bess and the ewe in order to compose an alternative text of their adventures. Extracts from this new text are then compared, in the plenary, against the original words of the book.

Re-read the last sentence on page 6, 'When the sheep were safe inside, Dad yelled, "BESS! BESS, COME HERE!"' and continue to the end of page 11, where Sam is having his hot bath. Discuss the fact that Sam is safe and warm and then turn the discussion towards Bess and the ewe. Explain that on page 11, although we hear Sam's thoughts, we don't know what Bess and the ewe are actually thinking or doing. Tell the children that they will be looking at the 'cold' pictures of Bess and the ewe in order to first tell and then write their story.

Starting with the frame of Bess and the ewe on page 10, use questions to establish what is going on in the picture. For example:
* What do you think Bess and the ewe will do now?
* Do you think they might be lost?
* Will Bess be able to get the ewe safely home?

Model how the story might start. It is very important to establish a narrative stance and story opener that the children will be able to sustain comfortably in their independent writing. Once the children have understood the task, ask them to help you to compose a few more frames orally.

Turning to page 10 in the Big Book, demonstrate how the story can be told in written form through shared writing. Give the story a title such as 'Bess and the ewe', and then on a piece of paper write down an opening sentence for the story. Fix the paper with Blu-Tack to the bottom edge of the page so that it is underneath the illustration of Bess and the ewe on page 10.

Move on to the next picture of Bess and the ewe on page 12 and repeat the process, involving the children in the shared composition and then continuing with the other Bess/ewe pictures in the book.

LESSON PLANS

GROUP WORK

Choose from the following two activities for children working in differentiated groups.

❋ Explain to the children that they are going to write their own version of the story of Bess and the ewe. Distribute copies of photocopiable page 30, 'The story of Bess and the ewe', and tell them that the pictures on the sheet show the key events of Bess and the ewe's story. Working either individually or in pairs in their groups, ask the children to carry out the following steps, using copies of *The Snow Lambs* to help them:

Cut out each picture on the photocopiable sheet.

Sequence the pictures and paste them in the correct order into their blank booklet.

Give their story a title.

Write their story of Bess and the ewe, trying to make their text 'fit' the pictures. (The last two frames of the sequenced pictures are taken from the main story to help the children to write a satisfying conclusion.)

❋ Invite the children to retell the story of Bess and the ewe, working directly from the book of *The Snow Lambs*. They can then be given the opportunity to tell it in the plenary session or at story time. Alternatively, they could record their retelling on tape.

EXTENSION

Groups who have completed writing their text about Bess and the ewe can take the opening frames and compare them to the original text in the book. What differences do they notice and why? Which version in their opinion is the best and why?

PLENARY

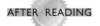

Start with the oral storytellings of Bess and the ewe. Focus on those children who successfully started the story in an interesting way and managed to include the main elements of the story structure, including the twist of the power cut and the resolution at the end.

Ask for some of the written versions to be read aloud, and respond to aspects which the children managed well, in addition to identifying any areas of difficulty. Monitor their success at managing sentence structure.

Invite those who were comparing sections of their story against the text, to read sample pages aloud and help them to summarize their conclusions. Encourage them to justify their preferences.

AFTER READING

CHARACTER PROFILES

RESOURCES NEEDED

Character word banks (see 'Group work'), photocopiable page 31, dictionaries; flip chart (with enlarged portraits of Bess and the ewe sketched on it in oval shaped frames), writing materials.

WHOLE-CLASS WORK

This lesson plan enables the children to review the main characters in the story. They build up simple profiles of the characters by extracting words from the text as well as supplying words of their own to describe the qualities of the characters.

On page 19, which provides a suitable context for this lesson plan, show the children the picture of the family sitting by the fire and draw their attention to the two pictures in oval frames on the wall. Who are these pictures of? Why do people put pictures of their family on the wall?

Show the children the portrait of Bess on the flip chart, and explain that through re-reading the book it will be possible to find words to describe Bess's character and create a profile in words about her. Re-read selected extracts from the book which provide clues to her character, and encourage the children to think about the words that might give clues during the reading. Take phrases about Bess such as 'That dog is useless' (page 8), 'What a clever dog' (page 30) and 'Brave Bess!' (page 31) to show how attitudes change towards Bess during the story (particularly in relation to Sam's father). Help the children to select the most important words from each phrase *(useless, clever* and *brave)*.

Discuss which words could be written around the portrait, looking at illustrations of Bess in the book to see if they provide further ideas to describe her character. What other qualities do the children think are important about Bess? (For example, her loyalty.) Write the chosen words and phrases around the portrait.

Now look at the character of the ewe, and look for clues in the book both in the text and pictures. The ewe isn't mentioned in the text itself until towards the end of the story, 'my best ewe' (page 30), but the reader can pick up clues about her character in other ways. For example, the final illustration of the book reveals her qualities as a mother. When key words and phrases about the ewe have been decided upon, write them around the ewe's portrait on the flip chart.

GROUP WORK

In differentiated groups, ask the children to work on a copy of photocopiable page 31, 'Character words'. This asks them to supply words and phrases to go around several portraits of characters from the book – Bess, the ewe, Sam, Mum and Dad – to compile a profile for each character.

Tell the children to look through *The Snow Lambs*, first for ideas and, where possible, to select words and phrases from the text. Explain that they should then describe the characters in their own words. They can use dictionaries, if necessary, to help them. For children who find the photocopiable sheet difficult, prepare some character word banks to support them.

When the children have compiled the 'character words', ask them to try to answer the question at the bottom of the photocopiable sheet: who has learned the biggest lesson? 'Learning lessons' is a significant theme of *The Snow Lambs*. Re-read page 8 with them, when Dad says of Bess: 'Maybe being shut out will teach her a lesson.' Then re-read page 30, which includes Dad's words: 'What a clever dog to bring my best ewe home to lamb!' Discuss how Dad's attitude has changed and why. Was he being fair to Bess when he shut her out? Help the children to compare possible answers. Ask them if they think anyone else has learned lessons in the story.

Finally, invite the children to turn the words that they have used in their character profiles into short biographical statements which could be presented in 'role' in the plenary. Give them a brief demonstration – an example might be: 'I am the ewe. Yes, I was foolish to wander off, but now although I'm tired and cold, I'm happy because I've had my snow lambs.' The statements could be keyed in on the word processor or handwritten neatly to be displayed with the profiles.

PLENARY

Select examples from the character profiles which can be used to draw out contrasts between the characters and possible contradictory qualities within them. Focus on those that have picked up clues from the text or illustrations and ask the children to explain how they achieved this. Draw attention to the power of descriptive words.

Ask some of the children to role-play one of their character's biographies, and if necessary demonstrate one first to give them confidence. Conclude by asking the class which character in the book learns the biggest lesson, and then demonstrate how Debi Gliori achieves this, looking briefly at the character of Sam's father. Refer back again to pages 8 and 30. Re-read Dad's words and draw out the shift in his attitude and what he has learned.

LAMBS AND LAMBING

RESOURCES NEEDED

The poster (All about sheep), photocopiable page 32, vocabulary cards, map of the UK, information book that contains a glossary, flip chart or whiteboard, printed copies of nursery rhymes about sheep, selected nursery rhymes on tape with headphones for children's use, *The Sheep-Pig* by Dick King-Smith (Puffin), Blu-Tack, writing materials.

WHOLE-CLASS WORK

In this lesson plan children are introduced to some of the less familiar but specific vocabulary used in connection with sheep, shepherding, lambs and lambing. Although some of the words will be familiar from reading *The Snow Lambs*, the children's understanding of some of them may only be partial, for example the phrase 'to lamb' used by Sam's father on page 30. The poster provides a context in which vocabulary can be introduced and meanings of words discussed.

The items on the 'All about sheep' side of the poster include a well-known saying, a sheep-counting rhyme from the Lake District and various labelled images to do with sheep. The use of vocabulary cards will enable the children to match words as they are introduced to items on the poster (these can be fixed on for display purposes using Blu-Tack). It is intended that the children broaden their experience by establishing links from the fictional world to the factual aspects of sheep farming.

To establish a context for the lesson plan, read from page 30 to the end of the book and ask the children to point out special words and phrases to do with sheep, lambs and lambing. Through shared writing, list the words on the flip chart. The list should include *shepherd, ewe, to lamb, newborn, bleating* and *lambs*. By looking at the final illustration, the children should be able to provide the word *twins*.

Next, explain that by looking at the poster, not only can many of these words be found but also other special words. Find examples on the poster, such as *fleece* and *crook* and explain their meaning. Using the vocabulary cards, ask the children to take turns to match them to words on the poster.

Through shared writing and with the help of dictionaries, show the children how to define some of the terms. For example, 'a sheepdog is a dog who helps a farmer to round up the sheep'. Compile a few definitions and then draw the children's attention to the glossary in the back of an information book and talk about why it is there.

Read the saying on the poster together ('Red sky at night, shepherd's delight, Red sky in the morning, shepherd's warning') and ask the children to try to explain it. Do they think the saying is true or is it folklore? If they do not understand the word *folklore* explain its meaning and give them some other examples of sayings, such as 'If it rains on St Swithin's Day, there will be rain for forty days'. Returning to the saying on the poster, do they know any received wisdom about sheep, for example 'counting sheep' when they can't sleep?

Finally, explain to the children that the story of *The Snow Lambs* is probably set in Scotland as that is where Debi Gliori lives. Locate Scotland on the map. Explain that sheep farmers all over the country have special ways of counting their sheep. Go back to the picture on page 3 of *The Snow Lambs* which shows Sam and his father counting sheep. Then on the poster, look at the Lake District counting rhyme, which has its origins in the Celtic language. Show the children where the Lake District is on the map and explain that this rhyme is very old, and that is why the words sound like a different language. Explain that as a bit of fun, you will teach them how to count sheep like a Lake District hill farmer. (However, they will be using their phonic skills to tackle these unfamiliar and apparently meaningless words.) Recite the rhyme, emphasizing the rhythm and the first, fifth and tenth numbers (in the Lakes, counting sheep in fives is important).

GROUP WORK

In differentiated groups, ask the children to work on one of the following tasks:
* Give out copies of photocopiable page 32, 'Sheep words'. Ask the children to match the words to the appropriate pictures.
* Ask the children to use the specific vocabulary given on the photocopiable sheet as a starting point for making a simple glossary.
* Help the group to compile a sheet which takes some of the vocabulary from the photocopiable sheet and lists the plural forms of the words (including regular plurals such as *ewes* and irregular plurals such as *sheep*).
* Give the children access to the poster to copy out the saying and illustrate it to explain its meaning.
* Let a small group of children listen to tapes of nursery rhymes such as 'Little Bo-peep' or 'Mary had a little lamb' and try to memorize the less familiar verses.
* If the children know *The Sheep-Pig* (or another book with a similar theme), discuss parallels that can be made between Dick King-Smith's book and *The Snow Lambs*.

PLENARY

Listen to some of the definitions written by the group working on the glossary. Provide input where necessary on the use of dictionaries for locating definitions. Ask the children who have worked on plurals to teach the group about the unusual words that did not obey the 'add an "s" rule'. Finally, establish some of the wider links with the nursery rhymes and some of the parallels between *The Snow Lambs* and *The Sheep-Pig*.

LESSON PLANS

WHAT ABOUT THE CAT?

RESOURCES NEEDED

Big Book version of *The Snow Lambs*, enlarged storyboard on the flip chart (the paper divided into six plain equal-sized boxes), photocopied blank storyboards, writing and drawing materials.

WHOLE-CLASS WORK

This lesson plan helps the children to recognize that often in story books there are other characters who have very different stories to tell besides those conveyed by the text.

Start by drawing attention to the cat on page 7 in the Big Book. Do the children notice it peeping through the window? Compare the picture to the text. Where is the cat mentioned in the story? Read on, and as the pages of the book are turned, see if the children can spot when the cat appears and what it is doing. Let the children see the cat's adventures in the illustrations and encourage them to notice how the cat's attitude shifts and changes as the story progresses.

Now use the enlarged storyboard to chart the start of the cat's story. Agree on the key points of the cat's story and make quick sketches on the storyboard, and through shared writing, ask the children to help to compose short captions to accompany the pictures. Focus on sequencing the key events of the cat's adventures in order to attain a satisfying story shape. Give some help and advice on selectivity. Then re-read the shared text.

GROUP WORK

Organize the differentiated groups so that they focus on different alternative stories (such as Sam's father's). The children within the groups can work collaboratively or independently on the task. Ask them to first look back through the book, discuss the illustrations and agree key points in the stories. They will require guidance on selecting the key points and clarifying the sequence. They should then compose their captions and illustrate them.

Children who need more support could have the main sequence of one of the alternative stories already prepared on their storyboard in pictures, thus enabling them to focus on the construction of the text. Rehearse their captions with them before they write them down under the appropriate illustrations. Provide the children with a personal word list of key words, if necessary.

Ask more independent children to plan and then draft their alternative versions of the story. The children should use a range of strategies to check their spelling and punctuation. A selection of the alternative versions of *The Snow Lambs* could be recorded onto tape and listened to at a later date.

PLENARY

Ask for successfully sequenced alternative versions to be read out to the class. Draw attention to the importance of sequence for the success of the story. From those children writing independently, select examples which have interesting or unusual openings to them and comment on this to the class. Finally, help the class identify some of the differences between these versions and the story as it is told in the book.

Name _____   Date _____

THE SNOW LAMBS (1)

✳ This story is called *The Snow Lambs*. What do you think the snow lambs look like? Draw a picture of the snow lambs.

✳ What do you think is going to happen to the snow lambs in the story? Write your ideas.

I think _____

_____

✳ Draw your ideas.

✳ Look at the cover of the book. Can you think of another title for the book?

I would call the book _____

✳ Why would you give the book this title? _____

_____

Name _____   Date _____

THE SNOW LAMBS (2)

The front cover of *The Snow Lambs* shows a picture of a boy and a dog with snow falling all around them.

snowflake

snow lambs

✳ Look at the picture and then make a list of all the words and phrases you can think of to do with snow and snowy weather. Write your snow words in the box opposite.

✳ What do you think the boy and the dog might be saying to each other about the snowy weather? You could use some of the snow words that you have collected to help you. Write their words in the speech bubbles.

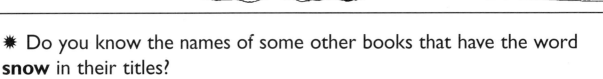

✳ Do you know the names of some other books that have the word **snow** in their titles?
Write your list below.

Name _____   Date _____

WHAT'S THIS STORY ALL ABOUT?

❋ Read pages 4 and 5 and look at the pictures. Then answer the questions.
Why is Sam's dad looking so worried?

_____

_____

_____

❋ What do you think Bess the sheepdog is doing?

_____

_____

_____

❋ Why do you think they'd be in
trouble if the tree blew down across
the power lines?

_____

_____

_____

_____

_____

Name _____   Date _____

WEATHER WORDS

✳ Read the first part of *The Snow Lambs*. Find the weather words and write them in the boxes.

✳ Look at the pictures in the book and see if you can make up some more weather words.

windy words	snowy words

What's the weather like?

cold words	cloudy words

✳ If you were Sam, how would the weather make you feel?

_____

_____

Name _____   Date _____

SNOW FACTS

✳ Read this piece from *Snow is Falling*. Put a line under any words that are similar to words that you have also seen in *The Snow Lambs*. You can use *The Snow Lambs* book to check for words.

Sometimes snow is not good. When strong winds blow, the

quiet, gentle snow becomes a howling blizzard. A blizzard

makes life hard for animals and people.

When snow gets very deep, the animals above ground can't

move about. Snow may cover their food, so that they can't eat.

Cars may get stuck and telephone wires may blow down.

✳ Make a list of any other similar words and phrases that you have found in *The Snow Lambs*.

✳ Write down three facts that you have learned about the snow.

1 _____

2 _____

3 _____

Name _____   Date _____

I HOPE...

✳ Find the three 'I hope' sentences and write them down.
The sentences have been started to help you.

1 I hope Bess doesn't _____

_____

2 I hope Bess can see _____

_____

3 "I hope Bess isn't _____

_____

✳ Look carefully at the three sentences. Two of them are Sam's thoughts and one of them is spoken aloud. Which one does he speak aloud?
Write your answer here.

_____

✳ Write down some of your own hopes for Bess in the thought bubbles.

Name _____   Date _____

WHAT DID THEY SAY?

✳ Write Bess and the ewe's words in the speech bubbles.

✳ Write Sam, Mum and Dad's words in the speech bubbles.

✳ Can you turn one of the speech bubbles into a sentence just as you would read it in the book? Don't forget the speech marks.
Write your sentence here.

_____

_____

Name _____   Date _____

THE STORY OF BESS AND THE EWE

✷ Cut out the pictures and use them to illustrate your own story of Bess and the ewe. Don't forget to make up a title for your story.

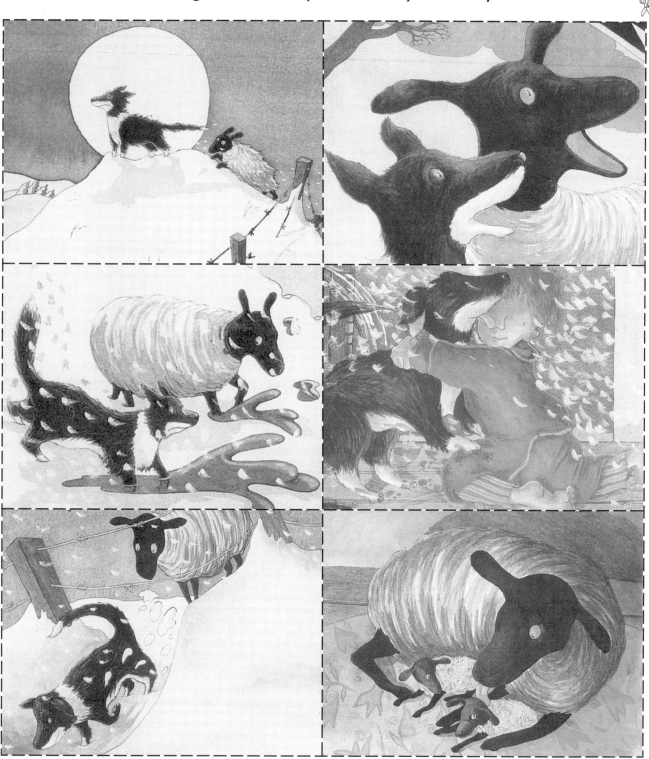

Name _____   Date _____

CHARACTER WORDS

✳ Write words in the boxes that complete the family portraits. Bess's portrait has been started to help you.

✳ Don't forget to use *The Snow Lambs* book to help you find words and ideas.

Bess	Mum
clever brave	

Sam	Dad

Ewe

✳ Who has learned the biggest lesson?

_____

_____

Name _____   Date _____

SHEEP WORDS

✸ Match the words to the pictures. One has been done to help you.

| sheep |
| wool |
| lambing shed |
| twins |
| ewe |
| ram |
| fleece |
| crook |
| flock |
| sheepdog |
| shepherd |
| lamb |

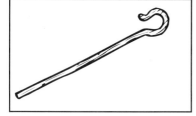